The 12 Secrets of Highly Creative Women
JOURNAL

Gail McMeekin, LICSW

Conari Press

First published in 2011 by Conari Press, an imprint of
Red Wheel/Weiser, LLC
With offices at:
665 Third Street, Suite 400
San Francisco, CA 94107
www.redwheelweiser.com

ISBN: 978-1-57324-494-7

Library of Congress Cataloging-in-Publication Data is available upon request.

Cover design by Barb Fisher
Interior by ContentWorks, Inc.
Typeset in Berkeley Oldstyle

Printed in the United States of America
MAL
10 9 8 7 6 5 4 3 2 1
The paper used in this publication meets the minimum requirements of the
American National Standard for Information Sciences—Permanence of Paper
for Printed Library Materials Z39.48-1992 (R1997).

CONTENTS

A Note to Readers . . . . *v*

First Gateway: Engaging Your Creativity 1

    Week One: **Secret 1**: Acknowledging Your Creative Self 3

    Week Two: **Secret 2**: Honoring Your Inspirations. 17

    Week Three: **Secret 3**: Following Your Fascinations. 31

    Week Four: **Secret 4**: Surrendering to Creative Cycles. 45

Second Gateway: Mastering Your Challenges. 61

    Week Five: **Secret 5**: Committing to Self-Focus. 63

    Week Six: **Secret 6**: Conquering Saboteurs 77

    Week Seven: **Secret 7**: Consulting with Guides 93

    Week Eight: **Secret 8**: Selecting Empowering Partnerships and Alliances . . . 109

    Week Nine: **Secret 9**: Transcending Rejections and Roadblocks. 125

Third Gateway: Actualizing Creative Results 141

    Week Ten: **Secret 10**: Living in Abundance with Positive Priorities 143

    Week Eleven: **Secret 11**: Subtracting Serenity Stealers. 157

    Week Twelve: **Secret 12**: Planning To Achieve Your Goals 171

Acknowledgments. *181*

A Note to Readers

WELCOME TO A new experience with the success strategies in my book, *The 12 Secrets of Highly Creative Women: A Portable Mentor*. I continue to get emails from women each week saying how much they love this book. Many have said that The 12 Secrets came to them at just the right time and spurred them on to take positive risks in their lives and bring their creativity forth into the world. I am deeply touched that my intentions for this book have come true and that Red Wheel/Weiser and Conari Press have continued to put the book into the hands of new women each year.

This journal is designed to inspire you further and urge you to take your creative dreams to the next level. You will focus on one secret per week, so the journal can be completed in 12 weeks. Or, if you choose to linger, you can do one secret per month instead. There are many 12 Secrets groups all over the world, so you can use the book and this journal to join one, start one yourself, get together with a creativity buddy and do the exercises together, or fly solo. Follow your intuition and do what feels best for you.

The discussions and writing prompts here are designed to deepen your intimate relationship with your creativity in your life, help you to embrace and commit to the ideas that are yours to express, and guide you in developing effective strategies to envision and achieve your goals. I developed many of these exercises in my individual and group coaching with creative women, and they work quickly and profoundly. I am happy to share them with you here. I urge you to take 30 minutes of quiet, reflective time each day for the 12 weeks/12 months to ponder the Secrets and make them your own. This is an advanced experience.

Do let me know what you discover. I can be reached at *www.creativesuccess.com* and I look forward to hearing from you. In the meantime, may the muse be with you.

Gail McMeekin, LICSW
Spring 2011

FIRST GATEWAY

. . . .

Engaging Your Creativity

WEEK ONE: SECRET 1

✿

Acknowledging Your Creative Self

LET'S BEGIN AT the beginning. You were born a creative child, with a unique personality and original ideas. The prompts in this chapter are designed to remind you of your uninhibited glee as a child when you learned to walk or hold a spoon or say your first word. You have always had the potential to be creative, to innovate and create something new and wonderful! We have lots of false myths in our culture that suggest creativity is an exclusive club for geniuses and the rest of us can never participate. Not true! Your creative self is alive and waiting for your invitation to evolve! It may be buried underneath fears of making mistakes, being rejected, or suffering from lack of attention, but your creativity lives! If you are in tune with your creative passions, these prompts will help you to discover new dimensions of your creative self.

This is a marvelous time to uncover your self-expression and your creative dreams. Imagine raking the leaves out of a flowerbed and discovering the buds of a stunning lady's slipper. That lady's slipper is your creative self. Get to know her, and watch her blossom big time.

❊ What are your unique strengths as a creative woman? We all have creative gifts, not just artists and designers. What are your gifts?

_____

_____

_____

_____

_____

_____

_____

_____

_____

_____

_____

_____

_____

_____

_____

_____

_____

_____

_____

_____

_____

_____

_____

_____

_____

_____

Remember back to those times when you were happy as a little girl. What kinds of creative play did you love to do back then? Are there any clues in that joyful play as a child that can serve you as a creative woman now?

When you were elementary school age, what things did you most enjoy learning about and doing? I know I loved finger painting, spending time at the library, and exploring the forest behind my house. I also loved reading stories about strong women. What were your favorite books, movies, music, and other activities at that age?

_____

_____

_____

_____

_____

_____

_____

_____

_____

_____

_____

_____

_____

_____

_____

_____

_____

_____

_____

✤ Who in your family was considered to be creative? Were they successful with their creativity? If so, describe their work and how it was received. If they were not successful or didn't reach their potential, what do you think happened? Be specific. What did you glean from these stories about the possibilities for you to have a creative life?

As a child or a teenager, what fantasies did you have about how you wanted to express yourself in the world? Were any of these fantasies encouraged by your peers, family, school, or other adults in your community? What kind of support did you get? If you did not get any encouragement, how did that make you feel about yourself and your ideas?

In junior high, high school, or college, what creative women did you know personally and admire? What creative women did you learn about through school, books, or movies? What was it about them that intrigued you?

What creative accomplishments are you most proud of? Describe
them in detail. What is the bravest thing you have ever done
creatively? What was the result?

WEEK TWO: SECRET 2

༺❧༻

Honoring Your Inspirations

TO ACCESS YOUR creative self, you must validate and capture your inspirations all the time. You need to continually honor the creative impulses that pop into your consciousness. I had a client tell me recently that she had a brilliant idea for a book while she was driving, but she forgot it. I told her that when she gets a valuable idea, she needs to stop whatever she is doing—even pull over, if she can, while she is driving—and write down her inspiration immediately so that it is not lost, and give thanks for her creative mind. Then, spend some time with this new discovery (either right then or schedule a time later to explore it). Your creative ideas are jewels—welcome them and take care of them.

Inspiration begins with *attractions*! Creative inspirations seduce you like a magnet. Diligently capturing your inspirations is a daring move and will place you on a new life path. The key lesson here is to value these attractions as the doorway to your creative self. How do you honor them? The first step is to cherish them as clues to your heart and soul.

For the first month of this journal program, write down everything that excites you—a word, a new coffee flavor, a tragedy, a magazine article, a nuance, a person, etc. I call this an Excitement List. Don't filter or censor your ideas, no matter how wild they may seem at first. Collect pictures from newspapers and magazines, the web, or take photographs of things that intrigue you and store them in the back of this journal for later. As the month continues, begin to notice your patterns of attraction—make note of them.

Keep asking yourself the following questions: What inspires me? What beckons me to explore it? As you move through this journal process, you will work with guidelines for sorting through your discoveries. Until then, trust that you are a creative soul scanning for a focus or a new angle on a focus you have already chosen.

✤ Create a sanctuary. It can be a room or a corner in your home, a meditative place in nature, a studio or office that you rent, or a quiet public place, like a museum or a library—anyplace where you can connect to your creative thoughts. Keep your commitment to spend 30 minutes per day with your creative attractions and study their messages. Rituals like lighting candles, reading, saying affirmations, using inspirational cards, etc. can fuel those creative insights. This is a time to experiment with leveraging what stimulates your creative energies. Also note what drains your creative energy or motivation as well. Use this journal page to record what you discover.

_____

_____

_____

_____

_____

_____

_____

_____

_____

_____

_____

_____

_____

_____

_____

❧ An essential part of the creative process is focus. You must ease up on your busyness and put a filter on all the external stimuli (information and media overload, etc.) coming into your sphere so that you can receive your creative impulses. How can you best set up those filters? Use this page to list the five or ten concrete things you will do to filter out excess noise. What will you say no to? When can you unplug?

❋ Find a symbol for your personal creativity and place it in your work/sacred space. It could be a shell, a book, a photo, a ring, a quote, etc. Touch it lovingly each day, and let it empower you. Write here why you chose it and how it is meaningful to your creative development.

❧ Collect objects (books, toys, statues, pictures) related to your inspirations and put them all together in one place to ponder for insights. So often, these objects can shed light and wisdom on our initial hypotheses and act as catalysts for new perspectives, novel strategies, and alternative paradigms. Write about the objects you've collected so far and what you've learned through the process.

Sit quietly, close your eyes, and picture your inner critic or inner critics. You are about to have a very important conversation with them. Say, "Hello. I am in the early stages of my creative explorations and I need to be free to experiment, make mistakes, take a wrong turn, and get lost. It is a part of the creative journey, and I need to make peace with it. Right now, I need you to be silent and not express your opinions about what I am doing. You might want to take a long vacation until I call upon you. Toward the end of my creative path, I will check in with you to see if you have valuable information for me that will help me to see things differently or more wisely. If you simply want to trash my ideas, I am going to shut down my communication with you, as our relationship needs to be built on respect. But this is not the time for mutual conversation and I ask you to abide by my wishes. Thank you. I will be in touch."

Make notes or draw pictures of this cast of characters, so that you know who they are. Give them names, and if they start chattering before you are ready, address them by name and tell them to be silent. You are in charge here.

❧ Go on adventures with your creative ideas. If you are writing about horses, go to a farm; if you are inventing a medical device, go to a science museum or a hospital; if you are designing a meditation room for a cancer treatment center, go and visit famous churches, monasteries, and natural wonders. Step into the environment of your ideas and immerse yourself in their taste, touch, texture, smells, visual effects, and sounds. You need to have a unique experience with your concepts. Write here what you learn from your escapades.

Week Three: Secret 3

༺✥༻

Following Your Fascinations

FOLLOWING YOUR FASCINATIONS requires experimentation and risk-taking. It means stepping off the safety of the shoreline and charting a new course. You may get lost, but you will learn something. You will progress, but your destination may well surprise you. Ah . . . that is the glory of the creative process. But this is where many creative souls lose their nerve and stifle their creative flow. Creativity requires a dance with your medium(s)—whether it's pastels, a business, or a social cause. Your creative dance may have a few standard steps. But to make it truly yours, you have to groove to the music in your own unique brain and make a new pattern. Your creative dance will have your signature on it, as will your final product or service.

❧ What truly fascinates you right now? It doesn't have to make sense or be connected to your creative project or your work. Select some way to learn about this fascination. Go talk to someone on the topic, surf the Internet for research about it, buy one, rent one, visit one, make one, and so on. Write about this fascination and why you think it calls to you. Its purpose may be unknown to you now, but someday you will remember this page.

What risks have you taken in life that have worked out well? Which ones have not worked out? What did you learn from the failed ones? What were your strengths and actions that made your positive risks succeed? Capture that wisdom here so that you can refer to it as you venture forth with your fascinations.

We have so many choices now about where and how to learn new skills. How do you learn best? Is your learning style visual, auditory, or kinesthetic? Do you learn by doing or by studying? Write down what you know about how you enjoy learning and the best models to stimulate your thoughts. What can you apply about your learning style to your creative fascinations? Where is the connection?

Travel enriches our lives and broadens our worldview. What are three places that you long to see? Write them down. Take some time to create a travel poster with pictures of those three places on it and put it somewhere so that you can see it each day. Find out how much it costs to go. Look up how you can get there and possible places you could stay. Make a mental picture of how you want these travel experiences to play out. Watch videos about your places if you can. Make sure you have the right three places picked out. When you know you do, make a plan—even if it is just having money automatically deposited into a travel account for starters. But be creative. Can you get there as a writer or photographer? Can you get there on a business trip by finding new prospects that live there? Are there volunteer vacations you can participate in? The more you work with picturing yourself in your special places, the more likely you are to get there—and soon.

Many women believe that the source of their creativity is their spiritual beliefs and practices. This spirituality may not necessarily follow traditional religion, as many women have left patriarchal religions to pursue their own spiritual path. What do you personally believe about your connection to a higher self or spiritual Source? How does that belief or lack of one influence your creative work?

Are you a solo creator, or do you create best with one or more collaborators—or some combination of the two? Which models have you have used in successful projects? Make sure you implement strategies that support your best working style. Record your thoughts about your creative style—about what works for you and what doesn't and why—here.

✤ What makes your heart sing with joy right now?

Week Four: Secret 4

Surrendering to Creative Cycles

HOW IS YOUR creative energy flowing at the moment? Are you in action mode or rest mode? Your creativity cycles through circles of birth, growth, decay, death, and rebirth. It has seasons just like the trees. What season are you in now?

Sometimes a creative block is simply a signal that it's time to rest and see what new callings find you! You do need to sort out that it truly is time to rest, not an excuse to procrastinate. In one of my recent workshops, a very creative woman interested in crafts commented that she was watching television at night instead of beading. She wanted to be beading, but she felt afraid that her results would not be "good enough." How can we get better at a craft if we don't practice it? I always ask people to consider what time of day their creative energy is most available. For many people, doing creative work at the end of a long day is unrealistic. But fear is often more of a creativity killer than fatigue.

Tune in to where you are in your creative cycle.

❧ Think about a time in your life when you were most creative. What fueled your flow? What kept you passionate and productive? When and how did you work? Where did you work? Make a list of all of the elements, psychological and environmental, that facilitated your creativity. Creative women often speak about being in the flow and actually mentally downloading their books, paintings, or designs from Spirit.

✳ Do you need to be in rest mode right now? Many creative women that I coach show up with one creative idea or a dozen, but they are buried under burnout and fatigue that need to be remedied. What do your body, mind, and spirit need in order to heal? If you need a spa weekend, a week at home to catch up, or a real sabbatical, do it now. If you do not take care of your physical body, it will not support your creative efforts.

Death, as a symbol, is a key part of the cycle of creativity. When we are done with a creative project, pursuit, or idea, we need to be willing to let it go. We may grieve or be relieved, but we need to remove it from our space and our psyche. I once finished a project that was grueling and when I was done, I gathered up all the files, the computer discs, and the notebooks and put them upstairs on the third floor and out of my sight. I had to hide them to free up new psychic space. What do you need to let go of or surrender? Many people hang onto their first idea and if they can't finish it, they don't let themselves put it aside and give it a rest. Sometimes, that is procrastination—maybe you are fearful of what happens when you get it done (and that is a different challenge). But sometimes we have something new that we need to experience or discover before we have the know-how to finish that old project. Write honestly here about what needs to be abandoned because it is healthy for you to do so versus what you need to buckle down and finish. Discernment and brutal honesty are key elements here.

_____

_____

_____

_____

_____

_____

_____

_____

_____

_____

_____

_____

If you think of your creative ideas as little beings, think about where they are in the life cycle of birth, growth, death, and rebirth. Most creative people have lots of ideas, hopefully captured in this journal, an idea book, or electronically. Selecting which ideas to infuse life into is a vital success strategy. Sometimes our ideas are ahead of their time, outdated, or too similar to something else that has been done. Who doesn't wish that they had invented the Post-it Note? Look back at your ideas in this journal and evaluate them using one main criterion: Do I have a *passion* for this idea? You can also ask yourself, Does this idea reflect my life purpose? Is it meaningful to me? Can I make money with this idea? Does that matter? We want to dance with projects we love, as our creative projects are real relationships. Which ideas do you feel like dating? Do those first.

Now, what if you pick your best idea that you are most passionate about and, after working with it for awhile, you decide you hate it? The first question you must ask yourself is, Is it real disdain, or is it fear? One valuable lesson I have learned as an amateur watercolor painter is that when a painting has gone off track and my efforts to fix it have failed, I need to let myself just trash it. I can sort out when I am being too much of a perfectionist about a painting or my writing and need to make peace with it until I get it right, as opposed to having created something that is not worth any more effort. We must let ourselves try, fail, and start over. If we are truly entranced with our idea, we will be more willing to fight for it. I felt that way about *The 12 Secrets of Highly Creative Women*. It began in the format it ended up in. But it also spent time as a novel about a frustrated writer named Brittany. My inner resolve was so strong that I kept reworking it while looking for the right publisher. How do you really feel about the idea or project you are focusing on now?

We have all heard the expression "being in the neutral zone," which means being in limbo, on ice, and a bit lost. We may be totally uninspired and have no brainstorms cooking in us at all. This is a time before rebirth. It is different from rest, because in the neutral zone we are usually searching for something, not just taking a time out. I see this state often in people who are changing careers and do not have a clue about what they want to do next. Also, creative people often work in many mediums and need to switch things up. I have a friend who is a very talented artist. She started out as an oil painter, switched to pottery and built a huge pottery studio, shifted over to landscaping, went back to oils, and is now in design school in love with watercolors and the Adobe Creative Suite. Her talent prevails, but she is continually intrigued by trying new forms of expression. There have been times when she has been in that "neutral zone" with nothing happening for her in the art world at all. She waits and listens and then follows the breadcrumbs to what is next. Are you or have you been in the neutral zone? What action steps have helped or will help you to move ahead?

❋ Is your creativity run-down and dilapidated? Are you in a place of scarcity about your creative expression? I met a woman the other day who is an interior decorator. Her studio was such a mess that you could barely walk around inside. She was complaining about the cost of materials and said she was now using inferior paints and fabrics and was disappointed by her results. While she had a studio, she didn't have an updated business card, let alone a place for a prospective buyer to sit and ponder her design work, which was haphazardly displayed. She clearly had talent and I loved her work, but her low self-esteem was blocking her prosperity. She needed to recreate her studio so that it supported her work and her wish to sell her services and products. She was cheating herself and her buyers by using cheap materials and not creating what she is capable of. Valuing her work, her talent, and the essentials she requires to make her design business self-sustaining and profitable is her challenge.

Are you shortchanging your creative process in some way? Are you giving your creative self what it needs to advance to the next level? Is there a teacher you need to study with? Are there quality products that you need to be buying to make your work more high-end? Are you underpricing your services as a result? Make yourself a creative project and invest in your development. Let your creativity enjoy a rebirth. Make a list of all of the things that you need to do or get to elevate your creativity to a higher level of excellence and fulfillment.

_____

_____

_____

_____

SECOND GATEWAY

. . . .

Mastering Your Challenges

Week Five: Secret 5

⟡

Committing to Self-Focus

YOU ARE A creative container, which is why it is so vital that you take care of your body, mind, heart, and spirit. Highly creative women take care of themselves holistically. They also have a regular schedule that puts their creative practice front and center in their lives. You cannot let your creative ideas and execution get lost on the bottom of your to-do list. I challenge you to put the action steps for your creative project at the top of your to-do list—not the bottom. Buy a groovy pen in your favorite color (mine is always purple) and write all of your creative goals in that color in your datebook or highlight them in your BlackBerry/iPad. When you evaluate your goals for the month, check out those color-coded creativity intentions. By focusing on you as a creative being with creative aspirations and putting that on top of your list every day, you will change your life.

Now, a note of reason. If you are the mother of a two-year-old who might eat a can of Comet while you are writing a poem or the caretaker of a person with Alzheimer's disease who might burn the house down while you converse with a gallery about showing your work, you need to delegate that responsibility to someone else during your creative time. I was once interviewed by a wonderful magazine called *Cape Woman* and they asked me, "Does creativity give you an excuse to be irresponsible?" In my opinion, we all need to be responsible to and for the people we have chosen to care for. Yet, we are also free to renegotiate the old "everyone or everything else first" model that the patriarchy prescribes for women.

However, if you value your creative gifts, you need to advocate for your creative time. You need to insist/negotiate with your loved ones your need for creative space. Self care, and making the time and the energy to fly with your creative ideas, is your right as a human being. Kindly advocate for yourself starting now and complete the creative project you have craved the time for. You and only you can make sure that it manifests. Change your focus to your creative fascinations and watch the universe support you in astounding ways!

What did you learn when you were growing up about taking care of your own needs as an individual and as a woman? Were you taught to "put everyone else first," or were you luckier than that?

❋ Are there any "shoulds" or perfectionist standards compromising your creative life? Write these things down here and make the decision to postpone, ignore, delegate, or ease up on yourself about them for now.

❦ What does your inner wisdom or intuition tell you about what
your creative self needs right now to grow and find fulfillment?

Do you need quiet time or solitude to get your work done? Do you need to get away and think, meander, or explore something compelling to you? If so, make a plan and negotiate for your needs. You deserve to get what you want out of life. Give yourself a better shot at completing the plan by writing it down here.

✤ Are there responsibilities in your life that you have outgrown or started to resent and that you need to give yourself kind permission to let go of? I had a lovely client many years ago who hated cooking the big Thanksgiving dinner every year. She found the whole ordeal of spending hours cooking (which she didn't enjoy), hosting guests, and then cleaning up hundreds of dishes and pots—not to mention the whole house—exhausting. We talked about it, and she quit. Now she either goes out to dinner on Thanksgiving or picks up food at a gourmet restaurant and brings it to someone else's house. She used to hate the whole month of November because of this "curse," as she used to call it. Now, she spends her November going out for hours at a time photographing the harvests all over New England.

What do you need to subtract from your life to make more room for your creative expression and the things and people that you care most about?

✳ In today's world, women are experiencing more equality and now make up half of the workforce. Yet, not all families are operating on the model of equality and are still influenced by old traditions, beliefs, and habits. The same can be true in the workplace, where women are still being underpaid. Are there issues at home or in the workplace that you need to renegotiate? If you value yourself as a creative woman, you may need to stand up for yourself, believe in yourself, and ask for what you deserve, whether that is more time, money, hiring people to help, more teamwork, more space, etc. Use the space below to list some of the issues that need renegotiating in your home and work lives. Then pick one issue at a time and start being assertive. People who really care about you will hear you.

Are you using both the right and left sides of your brain to help yourself set goals, make decisions that support your dreams, and stay in touch with your intuition? As women, we tend to see the big picture first and then we have to bring the ideas down into focused consciousness and blend the two domains. What is your style, and how can you leverage self-awareness to achieve both inspiration and completion?

Week Six: Secret 6

꧁꧂

Conquering Saboteurs

WHAT INTERNAL OR external saboteurs are interfering with your creative action? What negative voices or beliefs are causing you to doubt yourself? I see so many amazing and talented women stop themselves from achieving their rightful recognition because they feel haunted by fear and a lack of support. I call the haunting voices "spooks" because they scare us and eclipse the joys of a creative life. Their messages can make it hard to give yourself permission to experiment and try new things, which is essential to creative progress. Our 100th painting is so much better than our first, but we need to do them all to achieve the mastery and find the message that we want to communicate. These saboteurs often cause women to feel traumatized by one rejection or criticism, to the point that they'll hide their novel in the closet forever, swear they will never try to patent a product again, or promise that they'll never let themselves be vulnerable like that again.

Think about your spooks as personas in costume, dressed up for a sinister Halloween party. Write down the names of your top three spooks and study them. What costumes are they wearing? Are they ghosts from your past, like people in horrible high school cliques, grouchy teachers, unknowing or controlling parents, or misguided mentors? Are they negative folks in your current life whose messages about you feel like a punch in the gut? Or do you have inner spooks, like your own internalized slave driver who never gives you a break, or a fearful voice that says you have no talent?

Whoever these spooks are, take some time to write out their unsupportive messages on individual pieces of paper. Make a collection of these evil proclamations and set aside a night to burn them, saying the phrase, "I subtract your power from my life, as your message no longer serves me," as you drop each paper into the flames.

If your spook is your own inner voice, try to dialogue with it and find out if its message has merit. If it doesn't, ask your spook to leave you alone and go vacation in Antarctica until you call upon him/her for feedback or participation in your life. If they reappear from time to time, use "thought-stopping" (that is, ignore them and move forward). Fears so often camouflage brilliance. Let your creative essence shine through every day as you write in this journal.

❧ What talents do you have that you would like to share with the world? Don't be modest. Really tune in to what you are naturally good at, and give thanks for these blessings. Are these the talents you want to concentrate on in your life right now, or are there other stirrings you would rather explore? For example, I have a client, Suzy, who is a fabulous organizer for closets, offices, and homes. But she is tired of that use of her creative talents, and she now wants to use her organizing skills by working as a floral stylist, arranging flowers instead of "stuff." So she is taking courses and has a new mentor so that she can keep any "spooks" (who don't like us to change) at bay!

✤ Don't play small just so you can stay safe from the risks in life. There are spiritual penalties for not being on purpose. Claim your personal power and push through your obstacles. As we grow into a "bigger" authentic presence, we all have to try on new behaviors. The expression "fake it until you make it" means getting out there and practicing something new until you feel your message in your bones.

What if your wounds are so deep that you can't get out of the dark night of the soul? You may not be able to heal those wounds alone. So, follow your intuition and find healers who resonate with you. Begin to trust good people to help you face the spooks and reclaim your life. Self care and nourishing experiences like Reiki, massage, exercise, and meditation can also help you feel strong and centered again.

If you are playing with a new idea or direction in your life, gather your support system around you to listen and encourage you as you explore this new creation fully. Once you feel you have a grasp on your intention, call in someone to play devil's advocate and review your ideas with you. Tell this person that you are looking for objective questions and comments on your plans, not disrespectful input. If you choose the right person, you will learn something valuable that will save you time, money, and mistakes.

Many women are tormented by a fear of success. This fear may be related to the "imposter syndrome" that many women carry around, or to the fear of some of the losses that can happen when you are successful: a loss of privacy, vulnerability to criticism and rumors, or being treated differently than you were before. There are also tangled ideas out there that if you become well-known or wealthy you will no longer be a "good" person. Writing in this journal will help you sort out how you feel about your success. If you are struggling with any of these issues, ask your intuition to help you.

✤ If your spook's message has some merit, like "you don't know how to write a symphony or run a retail business," then create a learning path for yourself to get those missing skills. Successful people invest heavily in their own growth. It takes time and money to get really good at something.

To keep your spooks in check, think about teaming up with other positive creative women. You could find one person to connect with daily, and cheer each other on and soothe each other's angst. You could also gather a group of like-minded women together to start a *12 Secrets of Highly Creative Women* support group and use the book and this journal to do weekly exercises together and remind each other of your creative power and your intentions. The spooks get quieter when you drown them out with positive vibrations and the love of your soul sisters.

WEEK SEVEN: SECRET 7

❧

Consulting with Guides

THIS WEEK IS about consulting with guides. A guide is someone who sees who you are and helps you to find your way. Guides can be teachers, parents, relatives, mentors, psychotherapists, coaches, astrologers, psychics, shamans, friends, colleagues, organizations, communities, support groups, spiritual teachings, works of art, plays, movies, books, radio and television broadcasts, Internet information, chat sessions, or any other encounter with wisdom. My book, *The 12 Secrets of Highly Creative Women: A Portable Mentor*, is purposely subtitled "a portable mentor," as I interviewed 45 highly creative women to inspire and guide readers along their journey of creative discovery. The creative path can be lonely and fraught with arduous challenges, but help from guides can keep you centered and well-advised.

Books give us access to people we may not have the chance to encounter personally. Reading about inspiring lives is a great first step on your creative path. Take the time to identify people you admire and spend time learning about their lives. Remember back to real people in your travels who have supported your uniqueness and facilitated your growth. If you haven't thanked these guides in the past, now is your opportunity. If they are no longer living, honor them by writing down the powerful lessons they taught you, and thank them too.

If your life has shifted or you are feeling starved for new mentors, actively seek out new role models and advisors. Be cautious with whom you select, as not all guides can be trusted to honor your inspirations and allow you to follow your own path. Beware of anyone who wants you to do it only his or her way. Creativity is about *your* essence and *your* self-expression—not theirs.

What is your professional development challenge right now? Be as concise and specific as possible about the knowledge and training that you want and why. Think about formats and how you learn best. For example, do you want to take a class, work with a coach or a mentor, be in a group, do an intensive retreat, enroll in a degree program, do a joint venture with someone who has skills that you do not, join a professional organization, or do a self-study program with books, videos, etc.? Make a plan here.

Select the learning options that you think will work best for you, and then do your research. Above all, follow your intuition and only engage with folks that you truly resonate with. Your creative energy is precious and deserves respectful support and guidance. Keep in mind that you can also expand your own learning by guiding others along the way, too.

❦ There's an old warning that says, "Don't buy a car until you have driven it in the city and on the highway." Before you begin collaborating with another person, a group, or an organization, do a test-drive first. Don't join a professional organization until you've been there as a guest once or twice. Don't sign up for a long-term experience with a potential guide until you've had a few meetings to see if you click. Check out a potential teacher's website and even have a conversation before signing up for a series of classes. Write down the key attributes that you want a new guide to have and explore a number of options until your gut says, "Definitely yes!"

❧ We are so fortunate to be living in a time when, thanks to the Internet, we can learn from people all over the world. We can Google someone, follow them on Twitter, watch their videos on YouTube, read their articles on their website or blog, or participate in webinars with them. I always tell my clients to think of five people they admire who are doing what they want to be doing, and study them. Learn about their paths to success, their mistakes, and their advice. Who are your five symbolic mentors, and how will you access them?

You want to choose guides and/or learning experiences that focus on your primary learning style, but it's also good to mix it up to let your brain experience a range of input. Review any negative learning/mentoring experiences from the past so that you are clear about what you should avoid going forward. Then describe your ideal learning situation.

❧ Focusing on your project specifically, what are some of the tasks or subjects that are difficult for you to learn? Make a list. Now you have to make some choices: do you need to learn how to do all of these things, or can you delegate some of them to someone else and/or hire someone to help? If you decide to learn something yourself, how could it enhance your effectiveness? Be certain that it is worth your time and investment to learn it. I know a woman who was brought to tears while trying to learn QuickBooks®. She finally gave up, hired an expert to do it for her, focused on her strengths, and created a multimillion-dollar business. Don't get hung up on learning skills that are not worth your valuable time. You don't have to know everything about everything. Remember, there are certain skills, like self-marketing, that you can't delegate to other people. You need to learn from people whom you can communicate with well and whom you trust. Smart people learn from experts so they can shortcut the process and get to their goals faster.

_____

_____

_____

_____

_____

_____

_____

_____

_____

_____

Successful people know that they need to keep learning and growing constantly. Our world is changing at a rapid clip, and we need to keep up with it or we'll be left behind. Many successful people hire coaches or consultants to keep them focused on their goals. Good coaches and consultants ask tough questions, encourage creative thinking, and keep us accountable.

What kind of support and accountability do you need to live your vision and meet your annual goals? How much of that are you doing for yourself? Is it working? If so, great. But we all encounter obstacles and new challenges where we need some guidance. If things are not working and you are still trying to do everything yourself, isn't it time to stop and get some wise counsel? We all have things to learn, and we have to be honest with ourselves when we are stuck and need help. Carefully choose good people to help you to see what you cannot. Who might you consider for help now, or down the line? Write their names down here.

_____

_____

_____

_____

_____

_____

_____

_____

_____

_____

WEEK EIGHT: SECRET 8

〰️

Selecting Empowering Partnerships and Alliances

WHETHER OR NOT you work with others in your creative endeavors is a crucial decision that involves self-assessment and the careful selection of collaborators. For some people, working alone is a joy. For others, the isolation drains their energy and motivation, so they like to collaborate and create with other people. And still others like to start out alone and then build a team along the way. There are many possibilities. I've seen a common trend among women that can have disastrous consequences. I call it "the urge to merge." It's the idea that we are too scared to do a business/creative venture by ourselves, so we grab the nearest warm-bodied friend or acquaintance, and we go into business together without test-driving the partnership or spelling out all of the vital details of the alliance in advance.

When I talk with a client who has disengaged from a disastrous partnership or alliance, I ask her if there were clues that she overlooked. Generally, the answer is yes. Often my clients will say they "just had a funny feeling about her," they "didn't quite believe what the other person was saying," or they "wondered if she was setting realistic expectations for herself given her other responsibilities." Your intuition is a powerful gift; turn it up to full volume and listen to its wisdom. If you are even the slightest bit uncomfortable with the words or actions of a potential collaborator, pay attention. In any partnership or alliance, there will be disagreements and different perspectives. The question is, can they be communicated effectively and resolved, or not? Trust grows when both parties are equally committed to the success of the relationship and respect the feelings and thoughts of each other. Never work with people you don't admire or trust completely—it's a sure way to get burned. Honor yourself enough to choose people of integrity and good interpersonal skills to play with creatively. Then negotiate all the issues that need to be talked through to make sure that this alliance can be mutually beneficial. (Now seems a good time to mention that official legal business partnerships are different from alliances, which often do not have written contracts.) You want to avoid a courtroom. What are your priorities in choosing people to collaborate with?

✳ When two people consult with me about setting up a partnership/alliance, I give them the Myers-Briggs Type Indicator (MBTI) to help them zero in on their personal work style and their strengths and weaknesses, and I have them complete my Collaboration Profile, which is in chapter 8 of *The 12 Secrets of Highly Creative Women*. Then I ask them to write a brief business plan together with very specific info on work hours, investments and expenses, division of labor, etc. If they are still interested in working together, I then send them to a lawyer, an accountant, and the Small Business Development Center for input and advice. Only a few folks pass all of these hurdles and actually get together. Business partnerships break up more often than marriages, so proceed with caution. What assessment questions do you and a potential partner need to discuss?

Even if you've determined that you don't want an official business partner right now, you'll likely find that down the line you will want to or need to do joint ventures with others. The assessment tools I mentioned previously can help you make good choices about whom to collaborate with. Even if you are only doing one project with someone, you still need to be clear about who brings what strengths and liabilities to the alliance. It can help to have complementary skills, so that you get the advantage of diverse thinking. Positive alliances with people we enjoy can be fulfilling and a wonderful catalyst for creative invention.

Who are some colleagues that you would like to do a project or joint venture with right now? Make a list of them and then write down what you can uniquely offer to the partnership and what you hope to gain in return. Is it equitable? If so, great. But if it's not, how could you creatively make it work out so both parties feel like they've made a good deal?

Have you been a good partner in the past? When you were in high school, did you choose to do term papers or projects alone or with other people, when given the choice? Do you have a lot of enduring relationships, or are your relationships fraught with drama and disconnect? Do your relationships feel balanced, or do you feel that you give or take too much? Review what your relationship patterns have been like in your life, personally and professionally. Note how your style will impact any potential future alliances.

❧ Brainstorming, anyone? Having people to mastermind with about our creative projects or business can be invaluable if the timing is right and we are engaged with the right people. Do you have people as resources in your life right now who recognize your talents and encourage you to take the next leap? If not, then write about what kinds of individuals and/or groups you would most like to have as thinking partners for your work. If you do have one or more kindred spirits, are you happy with the way things are evolving or does something need to shift so that the value of this connection(s) can increase?

❦ What kind of a networker are you? Are you plugged into social
media, G-chatting and Twittering and Facebooking all the time,
or do you prefer face-to-face, in-person meetings and one-on-one
phone calls? Are you an introvert with a small, intimate circle of
connections, or an extrovert who thrives on big conferences and
lots of socializing? Your interpersonal style impacts how you share
your creativity with the larger world. Both introverts and extroverts
can be great collaborators and marketers. But you have to select
from the panorama of media and personal connection options
and find the model that you enjoy most and that works best for
you. Marketing and publicity are all about relationships, so being
a person of quality and integrity will serve you well. What is your
networking style right now? Is it effective?

_____

_____

_____

_____

_____

_____

_____

_____

_____

_____

_____

_____

_____

_____

_____

❋ Have you done collaborative creative work with a significant other or a close friend? How successful were those alliances? Some significant others can work together and thrive, while for other couples it is a disaster. Some friendships deepen through working with someone you care about toward a common goal; other relationships blow up, never to be revived. What do you know about yourself or your partner or friend that can guide you in making wise choices about working together or not?

Have you done a good job hiring people in the past, whether it's an executive assistant, a literary agent, or a landscaper? If so, what do you do well? If not, what do you need to get better at? Can you let people or connections go if they do not meet your expectations? Do you settle for just being supported, or do you have high expectations for the people who work with/for you? Do you take loyalty too far sometimes or simply resist change? Whether you are choosing a web designer, a company to license your work to, or an organization to be a spokesperson for, you must be discerning. Your reputation is at stake.

WEEK NINE: SECRET 9

Transcending Rejections and Roadblocks

ONE OF THE secrets of success is confronting adversity and transforming it into your next steps for progress. Too many women take one or two hits and freeze, unable to recover and forge ahead. When we are doing creative work, rejections and roadblocks are part of the program. Unfortunately, not everyone will like and "get" you and your work. It's a diverse world out there—we need to find the people whom we want to share both our creations and our personal selves with. Where are your like-minded others who share the same values and interests as you do? We all have to find these folks, our special audience, and it's not meant to be everyone.

When we receive a rejection of our work or hit a roadblock, we have some choices to make. I know, as a writer, that some of the rejection letters I have gotten have had an interesting point or two that I incorporated into my next proposal. Other times, rejection letters were boilerplate and not helpful at all—and I recognized that. Sometimes when you're marketing a product, like my Creativity Courage Cards, a store may reject you because they don't think their customers will pay the price you're asking for the product. That's good to know, because it means your product belongs in a high-end market. With many rejections, we learn invaluable and new perspectives on the marketplace.

As for roadblocks, like people who won't call you back, production errors in your product, or being stuck on a painting or your website design, we must persevere and use some creative strategies to loosen up our thinking and develop a new pathway.

❖ Make a list of strategies that will help you to stay confident and believe in yourself if you or one of your products or services gets rejected. This can include everything from calling a colleague to doing more market research, redesigning your pitch, etc. Do you need to take a break to clear your head so that you can come back better able to find new answers? Choose the strategies that will work best for you as you ponder a new plan.

✢ If you or your work gets rejected, how do you deal with your feelings? What kinds of conversations do you have with yourself about the value of you and your work? Did you do your very best, or could you have done better? If you did not embrace excellence, thank the person who rejected you and go out and create superior quality. If you did your best, behave lovingly toward yourself and trust that there is something better in store for you. Reaffirm your value and the purpose of what you are offering. Choose some kind of releasing technique like visualization, expressive art, kick-boxing, or writing to get those feelings out so that you can heal and think clearly again. Feelings of rejection need to be processed quickly so that you can get back into action!

✻ Once you have reaffirmed your confidence and released your feelings of rejection, put on your CEO hat. What personal strengths can you bring to this situation? Who can you talk to and get another perspective? If there is nothing to this rejection except a mismatch, then you can move ahead with your marketing plan with a few minor adjustments. If you have heard that you are way off course, and you determine that is true, you will need a new angle for getting your work out into the world. Write down all the changes that you think you need to make and talk it over with some people in the know. New beginnings happen all the time in a creative life.

❊ Write down three situations in your life where you dynamited through a roadblock or an obstacle of some kind, either personally or professionally, to achieve your goal. What was your formula for success? What was your mind-set? Did you have support from others? Did you use a special creative strategy? Celebrate your successes, and note your own recipe for getting what you want.

✤ What roadblocks or obstacles are in your life right now? Make a list. The first question is always, "Is the end result worth fighting for?" If yes, why? If it is not worth it to put a lot of your premium energy into mastering these roadblocks, it is okay to walk away. Sometimes, the things we give up on can make space for us to focus on what really matters. If we are going to embark on a campaign to overcome our roadblocks, we need to be committed. You must decide that you want the outcome enough to fight for it—or let it go, and find your dream elsewhere.

❧ Pick one roadblock in your life that you are committed to transcending. Write down why this is important to you, how it will serve you and others, what you want the outcome to look like, and your best strategies to accomplish this successfully. Then write a 5-step action plan with specific tasks and deadlines. Find someone who will keep you accountable and make a pact to keep you on track. This exercise is very powerful.

The world needs you and your creative inspirations. What needs to be healed in you so you will be better able to weather rejection and roadblocks gracefully and not suffer the pressure of not being able to please everyone all the time? As women, we struggle with this one. Find other creative risk-takers and support each other as creative women, who will fall down and need help getting up once in a while. If we are not failing, we are playing it too safe. Take smart, calculated risks in your life to reach your potential.

THIRD GATEWAY

. . . .

Actualizing Creative Results

WEEK TEN: SECRET 10

⚜

Living in Abundance with Positive Priorities

ABUNDANCE IS THE experience of plenty, often called prosperity. For creative people, the opportunity to dance with the creative process is itself an experience of abundance. Abundance invites us to live the life we truly desire instead of settling for less. We are the choice-makers of our own priorities. We do indeed design our own lives.

When I begin coaching a new client, I take them through a series of discovery exercises and conversations about what it is he or she truly desires. Determining our priorities gives us a roadmap for decision-making. Let me share an example with you. Sara contacted me a few weeks ago to help her change careers. She wanted to express her submerged creativity. She had read *The 12 Secrets of Highly Creative Women* and felt it was time to change her life. Sara's personal Positive Priorities, which I define in the book as "life choices that express who we are and what we want for ourselves," are:

- Having time to explore her creative potential

- Nurturing mutually beneficial relationships with others

- Maintaining healthy habits that support her body, mind, and spirit

- Keeping in touch with opportunities for learning about landscape architecture

At this point, Sara feels her creativity has been lost in a stressful job and a legacy of putting everyone else's needs first—in a city she no longer loves. Her number one creativity saboteur is guilt about finally defining and claiming her own definition of abundance. By celebrating her Positive Priorities, Sara now has a yardstick by which to measure her life choices up to this point.

Many of the women I interviewed in *The 12 Secrets of Highly Creative Women* had transformed their lives to honor their Positive Priorities. Sixteen themes emerged again and again, and I share them with you here to help you capture your own Priorities:

1. Time for creative exploration

2. Fulfilling work

3. Encouraging partners, friends, and community

4. Personal growth experiences

5. Good health

6. Nurturing living spaces

7. Learning opportunities

8. Self-protection from negativity and toxic people

9. Reflective time

10. Spiritual practices and beliefs

11. Independence

12. Solitude as needed

13. Inner centeredness

14. Connection with nature and the arts

15. Inspiring activities

16. Balance

❧ Look at the list of Positive Priorities and choose the ones that you want to be experiencing most in your life. Write down your top five Positive Priorities here and make this page easy to find so that you can refer to it daily. What time of day is best for you to take some time for yourself to reconnect with what you truly want? Schedule it every day for one month, for starters.

❈ Make sure that you are giving these Positive Priorities top priority in your life. Scheduling time for your friends, your art, or for exploring new business ventures should come first right now, not last. Notice your decision-making process for each Priority and what resistance/fears come up. If you want to do a craft or invent a new product this week, make it happen. Make these priorities a centerpiece in your life and your life will move in the direction of your desires. Learn to keep your commitments to yourself in the same way that you keep your promises to others. Write your commitments to yourself down here.

❧ What is your personal definition of heartfelt abundance? Which of your beliefs best supports this vision?

_____

_____

_____

_____

_____

_____

_____

_____

_____

_____

_____

_____

_____

_____

_____

_____

_____

_____

_____

_____

_____

What creative gifts and experiences are you most grateful for? How do you say thank you? I write thank you on the back of every check I receive and on the bottom of my website store shopping cart printouts, too. I also keep a gratitude list by my bed to write down the lucky moments in my life.

What is your mind/body/spirit/heart urging you to do now to take excellent care of yourself and spark your creative expression in the world?

❧ Are you doing what you love with your life? If not, what needs to shift?

✻ Who are the people in your life with whom you can celebrate your abundance? These are people who want you to have everything that you deserve. Be sure to connect with them regularly and acknowledge all the good things in your lives now and your aspirations for a prosperous future. Write down their names and say how you plan to stay in contact with them and offer support to each other.

Week Eleven: Secret 11

⚶

Subtracting Serenity Stealers

IN MY POSITIVE Choices stress reduction program, I coined the term "Serenity Stealers" to mean anything in your life that does not support your body/mind/spirit/heart. Serenity Stealers require what I call the "Power of Subtraction" to get rid of them. Your creative self is vulnerable and you need to vigilantly protect her, as she only has so much energy. As I write about in my book *The Power of Positive Choices*, we want to add Positive Choices into our lives—but first we have to make room for them.

Subtraction is like spring cleaning! Just as if you were weeding out your closet, it's time to seriously weed out your life to make room for new creative sprouts. To clear your creative channel, you must get rid of the things in your life that don't work and that compromise your creative power. This can include anything from old clothes to outmoded dreams.

Make a list of all your Serenity Stealers, those stressors that rob you of your centeredness and peace of mind. Then circle the top five. When confronted with a Serenity Stealer, you have three choices for action:

1. Can I avoid this, if I give myself permission to do so?

2. Can I modify this somehow to make things better? Tell the truth and at least consider the options.

3. If I can't avoid this or change it right now, what new coping strategies can I employ to minimize the impact of this negativity in my life?

✾ Now, take a second look at your choices. Most Serenity Stealers can be avoided or changed if you remember that you are in charge of your life. If your number one client is obnoxious, you can try negotiating with him or her. If that doesn't work, you can find some new clients. You almost always have options if you value your health and well-being and believe in yourself. If you seem to never have the time or energy for your creative project, you can take something of less value away from your life to make room, like friends you have outgrown, committees you don't want to be on anymore, or meaningless television programs. Look at what you can give up or delegate and then take action.

You have more power in almost any situation than you may realize or utilize. Write down all your options, even far out ones, to stimulate your creative ideas.

❦ If you are dealt what I call a "black card" in life that you don't have a choice about, such as a chronic illness, an unstable family member, or another challenge, such as dyslexia, you have to deal with it. But you still have choices about how you can cope. You can join a support group to help you with your illness, you can choose to not get too tangled up with that family member, or you can buy software that will help you with your spelling. The worst choice is to be passive and not advocate for yourself and your quality of life. If you feel stuck, reach out to others for a different point of view or support. Learning to release Serenity Stealers is a lifetime process. Begin wherever you can, and with each success you will be better able to tackle the really tough ones.

❦ Many of us as women have a hard time setting boundaries and saying no. If you have a hard time saying no to people's requests for your precious time, examine what criteria you are using to make decisions, and then examine your results. For example, if your Aunt Mary, your secretary, and your friend Leslie manipulate your time, then you can focus on how they push your buttons and plan your defense. What beliefs do you have about the value of your time and what you are entitled to protect in your life? Always remember that you are the creator of your own life experience.

_____

_____

_____

_____

_____

_____

_____

_____

_____

_____

_____

_____

_____

_____

_____

_____

_____

_____

❧ Think of a woman that you admire who seems to be in charge of her life and is living a creative and fulfilling life. If you can't think of anyone, start looking around you or read my book *The 12 Secrets of Highly Successful Women* for great examples. How do these women avoid negative stress in their lives? What do they feel empowered to do or say that you do not? Try on a new behavior this week of being honest and self-affirming in all your interactions with people. Treat yourself with respect, stand firmly in your goals, and connect with other people from a place of mutual respect and equality. Write down what you learn from your experiment.

_____

_____

_____

_____

_____

_____

_____

_____

_____

_____

_____

_____

_____

_____

_____

❦ Have you ever felt burned out? You don't want to get up in the morning, and the things in your life that once seemed important may have lost their meaning. Are you burned out now? Burnout kills our creative impulses, as there is too much sludge in the system for our ideas to emerge. They are stuck in the pain. If you or someone you know is feeling burned out, get guidance right away. The cure is exquisite self care. This means making key Positive Choices in your life and tuning in to what really makes you happy. It also means letting go of the people, things, and beliefs that can undermine your happiness. If you have a burned out friend, ask her how you can help, and encourage her to do what she needs to do to recover. In our 24/7 world, burnout for women is on the rise. How vulnerable are you, and how can you protect yourself?

In order for you to have the next level of success, however you define it, what do you need to change in your life right now?

Week Twelve: Secret 12

✤

Planning to Achieve Your Goals

OVER THE PAST eleven weeks or months, this journal, in combination with my book *The 12 Secrets of Highly Creative Women*, has outlined a process to help you to engage with your creative ideas and develop them into a passion, a business, or some transformation of yourself and your life. Now that you have discovered your inspirations, it is time to decide on some new goals and move forward to achieve them. You also need to make some critical decisions about whom you want to share your creative work with, and in what form. Are you doing

171

your creative work for pleasure or profit, or both? If you already own or plan to make a business out of your creative endeavors, what is your updated vision of business success? Not everyone wants to build an empire; many people want a simple life, and that is their top priority. Write down both your personal and professional goals with deadlines here. To be effective, your goals need to be specific, measurable, realistic, recorded, time-targeted, and Positive Action-oriented, with steps for following through.

Two key ingredients in the goal-setting process are commitment to what you desire and focus. Many creative people suffer from what is called "Ideaphoria"—an abundance of ideas. This is both a gift and a curse. I know, as I am in the 99th percentile on Ideaphoria skills. Like many of you, I have more ideas than lifetimes.

Many creative people operate under an "expansive umbrella," where they link multiple ideas together and work in a big-picture arena. First, though, we need to choose one thing to focus on and experience the power of completion. From there, we can move on to linking our completed projects under a central theme or experience, with each one being a completely new learning adventure. Declare in writing your "expansive umbrella" creative goal. What common theme ties together all of the unique things that you do? The world needs your creative brilliance—please share it with us!

❧ Select a creative project to complete that is heartfelt and inspires passion in you. Write down an action plan step by step. Support your vision with pictures and props to help you to achieve this goal. Then pull together a team of fabulous people to cheer you on and advise you along the journey.

Spend five minutes each day visualizing the satisfaction of achieving your goal and completing your special project. Tune in to your personal creative mission and purpose for your project and write about what creative wisdom you gain from this experience here.

When you have achieved your goal, plan a celebration and revel in your new sense of creative power. You have become a creative person who keeps commitments to yourself and others, and your life will never be the same. Claim your creative high points and build on them!

_____

_____

_____

_____

_____

_____

_____

_____

_____

_____

_____

_____

❋ Even if you are resting or in the neutral zone in your chosen field, what creative outlet will keep you engaged and expressing yourself right now? I know a sales executive who is spending time making special sauces and a lawyer who is volunteering at a dog beauty parlor and loving it. Often, our fun projects that we naturally pursue while we are in transition help us to uncover a new dimension of ourselves. Will they lead to a new career or creative path? Maybe, maybe not—it may just be an opportunity to satisfy a fantasy, and that's wondrous enough.

✳ Write a heart-centered mission statement about your creative intentions going forward, and say why this commitment is important to you. What are you trying to express? What form will it take? And how does it serve the planet? Add anything else that feels important to include. Make this a meaningful paragraph, and refer to it often.

Procrastination may be caused by indecision, having the wrong goal or plan, or trying to solve the wrong problem. We have to blast through it, though, to achieve our goals and dreams. So find a person to brainstorm with who has your best interests at heart, and wrestle your procrastination issues to the ground and see what decisions you need to make to move ahead. If you are committed to your project and are on the right track, then you just need to begin. Set a timer for 20 minutes and start—no excuses. Even if you just sit there thinking but not acting, the momentum has begun.

❦ Quite often, when we tap into our mission for our creative work and make a spiritual connection with our audience, our work becomes guided and far easier. Whom do you want to share your creative work with? How can you connect with them in a way that feels right to you? Honor your personal communication style and come up with a plan that expresses who you are in the world. Write down your thoughts about this and choose the best options for you.

❀ You have the power to be a highly creative woman. Your life is a work of art, and you are the sculptor who fashions it and crafts the vision that you see for yourself. Go forth and step into your vision now.

Acknowledgments

I HAVE TO first thank the thousands of readers of *The 12 Secrets of Highly Creative Women* who kept writing to me for ten years telling me that they would like to have a journal to go with the book. Secondly, I have to thank Caroline Pincus, my editor, for saying, "Of course— let's do that!" It is because of her that this long-time dream of mine and yours, my readers, rests in your hands. Thanks to the entire team at Red Wheel/Weiser and Conari Press for their wizardry at bringing beautiful, intelligent books to their readers. I feel so blessed to be part of this family. Lastly, I have to express my gratitude for my Ideaphoria, which seems to be tapped into some divine well which overflows with a myriad of ideas to share with you. It is a miraculous connection to my inner wisdom and my creative soul and makes creating books and products a joyful experience.

ABOUT THE AUTHOR

 GAIL MCMEEKIN is the founder and pres-
ident of Creative Success, LLC and the author
of *The 12 Secrets of Highly Creative Women*, *The
Power of Positive Choices*, and *The 12 Secrets of
Highly Successful Women*. Her work has been
featured in Redbook, The Boston Globe,
Health, Investor's Business Daily, and other
national publications, and she is a frequent
guest on radio and television. McMeekin holds
an MSW from Boston University, a certificate in Human Resource Man-
agement from Bentley College, and completed the coursework for the
Coaches Training Institute. She lives in the Boston area. Visit her at
www.creativesuccess.com.